VIAGRA
NATION

VIAGRA NATION

BY BRUCE McCALL
AND LEE EISENBERG

📖 HarperPerennial
A Division of HarperCollins*Publishers*
http://www.harpercollins.com

HarperPerennial

A Division of HarperCollins*Publishers*

FIRST EDITION

ISBN 0-06-019311-5

98 99 00 01 02 / 10 9 8 7 6 5 4 3 2 1

DEDICATION

In June 1998, Alan C. ("Ace") Greenberg,
chairman of the investment firm Bear Stearns,
personally donated $1 million to the "Viagra needy":
people who can use a lift but can't afford the price
of emission. Ace, this book's for you.

WARM-UP EXERCISE

Starting this book cold can be dangerous! You might pull a muscle — or worse. So get the blood moving by taking a moment to fill out this nakedly prurient questionnaire.

1. I am buying this book for myself ❑ a friend ❑ a friend of a friend ❑ a cousin ❑.

2. Does your "friend" or "friend's friend" or "cousin" very closely ❑ incredibly closely ❑ identically ❑ resemble you?

3. I first heard about Viagra from: my cellmate ❑ Voice of America ❑ a passerby ❑ don't know ❑ don't care ❑ know but don't care ❑ care but don't know ❑.

4. I hope Viagra makes my friend's/friend of a friend's/cousin's sexual performance better ❑ worse ❑ than: powdered rhino horn ❑ tiger's milk ❑ oysters ❑ cocktails ❑ and in fact leads him to experience the following degrading sexual situation (describe vividly):

_____

_____

5. I prefer that "his" degrading experience first be revealed to family ❑ friends ❑ boss ❑ Interpol ❑ Jerry Springer ❑ Kenneth Starr ❑.

6. I am already ❑ not yet ❑ a Grand Prize winner in the official $50 billion "Waiter, There's a Viagra in My_____" sweepstakes. Win or lose, I hereby authorize Ed McMahon, Dick Clark, Zsa Zsa Gabor, the Monkees and/or John Madden to smash down my front door on national TV.

"It's a great drug."

– Bob Dole

CONTENTS

FOREPLAY

VIAGRA: THE CLIMAX OF MAN'S MILLION-YEAR QUEST

In the beginning was the Big Bang, now estimated to have occurred on the night of Adam and Eve's first date. Man's sense of sexual security has been softening ever since.

1,000,000 B.C.: Intimidated by his mate's constant and unflattering comparisons of him to a woolly mammoth, primitive man learns to be defensive about his relative masculinity and potency.

Early Cave Painting

Ancient Egypt: Geti-Tup, 32nd pharoah of the Ha Dynasty, runs personal ads on his temple walls, but to no avail. He dies without an heir.

Section of Temple Wall in Geti-Tup Dynasty

500 B.C: Male inadequacy becomes a running joke in ancient Greek art.

Greek Urn, circa 425 B.C.

323 B.C: War, plagues and unlit cellar stairs make life expectancy short for all humans. During this dark age before dating, drive-in movies and other lifesaving sexual "safety valves," Alexander the Great — like many other males under thirty — dies from the ravages of acute puberty.

1575: Dirty-minded church censors force John Donne to change a line in one of his greatest works, from "Every man is a peninsula" to "No man is an island." Male pride is stunted at every turn.

1650: The nadir of male sexual confidence is reflected in fashion. Men go around in girly wigs and velvet suits with lacy ruffles everywhere.

Portrait of Rocky Quatorze, Heavyweight Champion du Monde, 1653

1796: Swinging bachelor Thomas Jefferson invents the girlfriend after publicly hanging out with Sally Hemings but declining to marry her. This makes it OK to hit on women other than one's wife or intended, which vastly expands men's potential sexual relationships. But liberation backfires: men feel more threatened than ever because there's more pressure to perform.

1863: His sexual amour propre sagging, the American male seeks solace in aggressive – but harmless – symbols. A pathetic example is his hat. The original domed-shaft design would be sanitized until it became the innocuous "stovepipe," fit to be worn in polite society by such as President Lincoln.

SEXUAL DESIRE IN THE AMERICAN MALE FROM PUBERTY TO SENILITY (PRE-VIAGRA)

Prior to the little blue pill, the fevered sexual enthusiasm of adolescence soon spent itself and men's expectations of satisfaction shrank until they faced old age with nothing to look forward to.

1902: Teddy Roosevelt popularizes credo "Walk softly and carry a big stick." "Easy for him to say," carp hoi polloi.

1905: A startling evolutionary "missing link," the Cardiff Giant, is unearthed in England. This oldest human skeleton ever found clearly shows that earliest man carried a giant three-foot-long club that doubled as his phallus when screwed into the pelvic socket. Male pride swells with the knowledge

KEEPING A STIFF LOWER LIP
HOW THE BRITS SCREWED THINGS UP EVEN FURTHER

The tradition of sending British lads off to boarding school at age six or seven, and leaving them there for the next ten or more years, denied generations of Anglo-Saxon males the female contact that leads to unraveling the mysteries of sex. As a result, the average Harrovian or Etonian was doomed to stumble from puberty to senility in a fog of sexual ignorance and confusion.

The British male's energies went instead into empire building, military adventure and trade abroad, and into horsemanship, shooting and politics at home. Overseas, that ingrained ignorance and fear of sex led to tensions and ugly incidents. In Victorian-era India, for example, a few virile sepoys attempted to demonstrate male sexual that except for some silly Darwinian wrinkle all men could be three-footers. Then it instantly deflates when the "missing link" is exposed as a hoax perpetrated by an embittered paleontologist whose police medical exam described him as "hung like a hamster."

1948: Alfred Kinsey's report on human sexuality renders the missionary position obsolete overnight. What to do?

1955–75: The deteriorating state of heterosexual man's

endowment to their British masters by taking off their clothes, looking at portraits of Princess Alexandria, and letting nature take its course. This so-called Sepoy Uprising was cruelly quashed. At home, male sexual confusion also exacted an embarrassing toll. Six successive royal weddings were abruptly canceled after the princes' brides-to-be were identified as boyhood boarding-school chums.

Only as the Victorian period ended and transcripts of Oscar Wilde's notorious trial were circulated did Englishmen awake at last from their asexual stupor. Their ensuing national fascination with big guns — with anything long and powerful that went bang — has been blamed for the nation's fateful plunge into World War I and the carnage that followed.

SEXUAL SELF-ESTEEM AMONG AMERICAN MALES BY PROFESSION

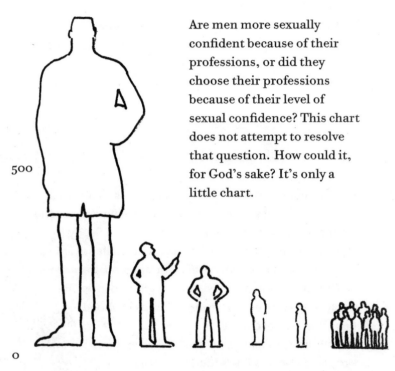

1000

500

0

Are men more sexually confident because of their professions, or did they choose their professions because of their level of sexual confidence? This chart does not attempt to resolve that question. How could it, for God's sake? It's only a little chart.

NBA PLAYER   ACTOR   PERSONAL TRAINER   CPA   DENTIST   ALL OTHERS

self-esteem is mirrored in a succession of entertainment idols: Liberace, Johnny Mathis, Tiny Tim and Michael Jackson.

1976: Presidential candidate Jimmy Carter confesses to feeling sexual lust in his heart, but his effort at hotting up his bland image fails: a national poll finds that women haven't noticed. Carter is elected anyway.

1977: Feeling themselves represented by a sexual cipher in the White House, American men are forced into disco life for solace. The culture hits rock bottom.

1978: The film *Urban Cowboy* is released. Women's primary sex object switches from men to mechanical bulls.

1996: Good news for a change! After even the cutesy Brit sex idol, actor Hugh Grant, is revealed to have solicited sex for money, the ancient shame of "paying for it" virtually evaporates.

1997: Bad news is back. A mighty Jakarta skyscraper fails to reach full erection before it spectacularly collapses — renewing male agonies of self-doubt in a thud heard 'round the world. The bigger they are, seems to be the moral, the more publicly they fail.

1998: Viagra!

PART I

HOW VIAGRAN ARE YOU?

DO YOU REALLY NEED VIAGRA?
A SIXTY-SECOND TEST

1. Do you think about baseball during sex? YES ❑ NO ❑
Do you think about sex during baseball? YES ❑ NO ❑

2. Which of the following is correct?

a. b.

3. When you mentally undress a woman, you always like to:
- ◆ Neatly fold her stockings
- ◆ Check for birthmarks, pimples, unsightly body hair
- ◆ Give her a screen to stand behind
- ◆ Keep your eyes tightly closed

4. You are a forest ranger, up for reassignment. Which tree type do you feel best suited to work with?

Redwood   **Young maple**   **Japanese bonsai**

5. Men over twenty-five who French-kiss their mothers are:
- ◆ Testosterone imbalanced
- ◆ Sick little twits
- ◆ French

6. If your lovemaking were interrupted by Nazi storm troopers breaking down the door, you would:
   - ◆ Protest to your building's superintendent
   - ◆ Ask your partner for a rain check
   - ◆ Break out the Uta Lemper records

7. Which date most closely coincides with your last satisfying sexual experience?
   - A. Last year's office party
   - B. Don Larsen's 1956 perfect game
   - C. Last year's county livestock show
   - D. Tuesday night's AOL chat room

8. You often lie about your sexual prowess to:
   - ◆ Total strangers
   - ◆ Yourself
   - ◆ Both of the above

   If both of the above, how often do you have sex?
   Check one:
   Daily ❑   Twice weekly ❑   Once a month ❑
   Really ? ❑   *Really?* ❑

If you completed all questions without an erasure, congratulations – you're a Viagran!

BRAIN ACTIVITY
OF TYPICAL VIAGRA NON-USER

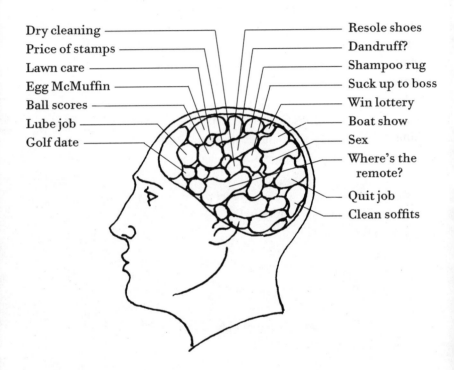

Dry cleaning

Price of stamps

Lawn care

Egg McMuffin

Ball scores

Lube job

Golf date

Resole shoes

Dandruff?

Shampoo rug

Suck up to boss

Win lottery

Boat show

Sex

Where's the remote?

Quit job

Clean soffits

BRAIN ACTIVITY
OF TYPICAL VIAGRA USER

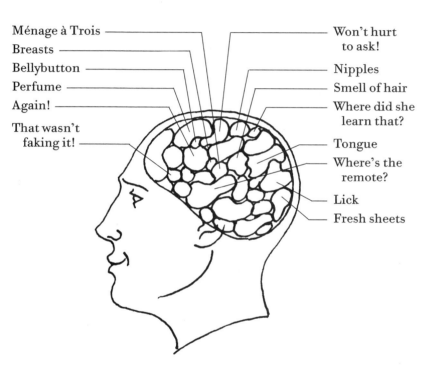

Ménage à Trois

Breasts

Bellybutton

Perfume

Again!

That wasn't faking it!

Won't hurt to ask!

Nipples

Smell of hair

Where did she learn that?

Tongue

Where's the remote?

Lick

Fresh sheets

VIAGRA COUNTRY

Increased hydraulic force behind the love-piston? Ninety percent more compression load on the penile mainspring? Six sections added to the telescoping male mainmast?

As far as the average man is concerned, what's it matter if one knows or doesn't know what makes him and his partner tick? All that counts is going from "ho hum" to "Holy Hector!"

Yet understanding Viagra's chemical wizardry and the male and female bodily systems it affects – just like understanding how those hooks work on the back of the brassiere, or how to find your Palm Pilot in the dark – can actually deepen pleasure.

As for the scientific principles behind Viagra: imagine shooting so much water into a dead garter snake that it stretches to the length of an anaconda, and you've got it. The male and female "equipment" can be just as readily grasped. The easy-to-explain diagrams on the following pages have been custom-prepared from the familiar masculine point of view, by men just as sensitivity-resistant and low-rated in sexual IQ as you are. If you don't understand a diagram, or have trouble figuring out big words, simply whine and rant as usual; your lover/mate/partner/spouse/mother will come and fix it, like always.

MAN LOOKS INTO MAN

(AND FINDS A '78 CAMARO)

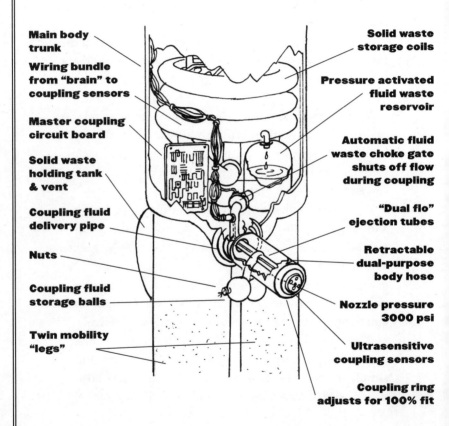

Main body trunk

Wiring bundle from "brain" to coupling sensors

Master coupling circuit board

Solid waste holding tank & vent

Coupling fluid delivery pipe

Nuts

Coupling fluid storage balls

Twin mobility "legs"

Solid waste storage coils

Pressure activated fluid waste reservoir

Automatic fluid waste choke gate shuts off flow during coupling

"Dual flo" ejection tubes

Retractable dual-purpose body hose

Nozzle pressure 3000 psi

Ultrasensitive coupling sensors

Coupling ring adjusts for 100% fit

VIAGRA COUNTRY
MAN LOOKS INTO WOMAN
(AND FINDS HIMSELF AT SEA)

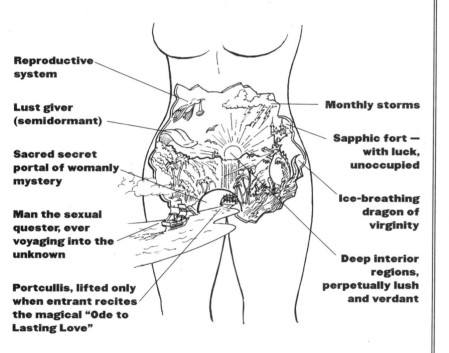

Reproductive system

Lust giver (semidormant)

Sacred secret portal of womanly mystery

Man the sexual quester, ever voyaging into the unknown

Portcullis, lifted only when entrant recites the magical "Ode to Lasting Love"

Monthly storms

Sapphic fort — with luck, unoccupied

Ice-breathing dragon of virginity

Deep interior regions, perpetually lush and verdant

THE WADD RATING:
HOW POTENT IS POTENT?

The Wadd* is science's first precise measurement of ejaculatory force. Like its close relative the watt, the Wadd is a unit of energy – in this case, sexual energy. Simply put, the more Wadds generated, the more ardent the sexual performer.

Superseding such obsolete folk sayings as "It ain't the meat, it's the motion" and "the heat of the meat equals the angle of dangle," the scientific Wadd Rating formula combines pounds per square inch of fluid pressure as measured exiting the male coupling-device hose tip (see diagram, p. 30).

Establishing accurate Wadd Ratings is no simple task – nor one without pain. The measurement equipment itself, consisting of multiple catheters, needles, clamps and implanted sensors with accompanying filaments and wires and coils, has been rated equal in the generation of physical pain to penile hammering on a sizzling griddle during bouts of severe toothache.

* The term "Wadd" derives neither from the late celluloid idol Johnny Wadd nor from the English inventor James Watt. The name is an acronym for Wisconsin Ardency Determinant Diagnosis, which reflects its origins in basic research at the University of Wisconsin's Advanced Sexual Propulsion Laboratory.

STIMULI FOR ERECTILE FUNCTION

Viagrans and non-Viagrans alike respond at precisely
the same speed and with precisely the same Wadd Index
(measured in degrees above the horizontal) when
exposed to these classic stimuli:

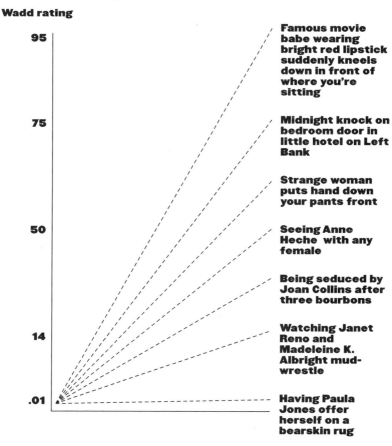

Wadd rating

95 — Famous movie babe wearing bright red lipstick suddenly kneels down in front of where you're sitting

75 — Midnight knock on bedroom door in little hotel on Left Bank

— Strange woman puts hand down your pants front

50 — Seeing Anne Heche with any female

— Being seduced by Joan Collins after three bourbons

14 — Watching Janet Reno and Madeleine K. Albright mud-wrestle

.01 — Having Paula Jones offer herself on a bearskin rug

SO, HOW VIAGRAN ARE YOU?

Post-Viagra findings that as many as thirty million American males suffer from some degree of erectile dysfunction have quickly unzipped the once taboo subject of impotence and unbuttoned the myth behind which it so long lay coiled, limp and untouched.

Thanks to the Wadd Rating, science can now classify and categorize every adult male's sex drive according to actual criteria.

How Viagran are you?

The levels are listed below. Read 'em and weep — or leap!

BASIC WADD RATING CHART:

100: Extreme satyriasis

50: Median honeymoon performance

0: Average for couple married 10+ years

100: FULL-BORE VIAGRAN — Your megapotency is a local byword: graffiti artists you don't even know spray your exploits on subway cars and bridges. Bag ladies follow you home. Maiden aunts send you Viagra sachets as birthday gifts. You haven't had time to make your bed in months.

90: RECREATIONAL VIAGRAN – You're only selectively potent – weekends, vacations, once a day or so. Hours pass when you feel no tightness or discomfort in your trousers. Forced to choose between having sex and meeting the president of the United States, you'd make the president wait only half an hour.

80: PROVISIONAL VIAGRAN – You don't stash *Hustler*s in the bathroom magazine rack; no need. True, your last girlfriend decided to go with a college basketball player about to be drafted by the pros – but the decision took her weeks. You feel pity for male strippers who stuff sweat socks in their trunks. You turned off the O.J. slow-speed chase so you could "have a go."

65: BORDERLINE VIAGRAN – You'd like to "get it on" with two girls at once but don't quite have the nerve to try arranging it and are too proud to hire professionals. You always have to say "Just a minute!" and get up and walk around first when someone calls you while you're watching *Ally McBeal.* Alone last summer at the beach, you preferred reading the new Tom Clancy novel to rereading *The Story of O.*

50: APPRENTICE VIAGRAN – Your dad took you to a hooker on your fortieth birthday. You worry whether your underwear is frumpy. When women in deep décolletage bend over, you look the other way. Nothing happens "down there" when you're looking into your neighbor's bathroom through your infrared nightscope.

40: DWEEB VIAGRAN — The only blind dates you can get are with blind girls. At the beach, complete strangers bury you in the sand. Every time you wear a raincoat the cops follow you. You go home early from your own birthday parties. You have the feeling that teenage girls are sneering at you. You've visited the adult section of your neighborhood video store five times without ever taking a selection home.

20: WET NOODLE VIAGRAN — You think "fellatio" is the name of an Italian film director from the late fifties. You wear button-fly trousers. You stopped sleeping with Mom only when your dad came home early from a business trip. When you mentally undress a woman, you only get as far as her wristwatch.

SPECIAL USER GROUP INSTRUCTIONS
INDICATIONS AND CONTRAINDICATIONS

VOYEURS Do not ingest Viagra yourself. Instead, forty-five to sixty minutes before their lovemaking is due to commence, slip a Viagra tablet into the drinks of the couple you intend to watch. If they are over seventy, take a No-Doz. If you are over seventy, take two No-Doz.

FLASHERS Swallow Viagra tablet approximately sixty minutes before donning raincoat. Good news: use of Viagra may actually draw a crowd. Bad news: you may not stand out in that crowd.

BULIMICS Swallow one tablet on an empty stomach ten to fifteen minutes before instigating regurgitation to eject it. Note: failure to eject tablet is harmless. Viagra contains zero calories.

DYSLEXICS Xes erofeb telbat eno. Sey, dogymho, sey, sey!

NEUROSEXUAL WIRING DIAGRAM
OF TYPICAL MALE
(PRE-VIAGRA)

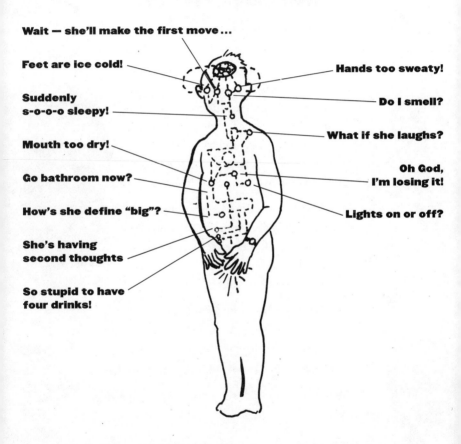

Wait — she'll make the first move ...

Feet are ice cold!

Suddenly
s-o-o-o sleepy!

Mouth too dry!

Go bathroom now?

How's she define "big"?

She's having
second thoughts

So stupid to have
four drinks!

Hands too sweaty!

Do I smell?

What if she laughs?

Oh God,
I'm losing it!

Lights on or off?

NEUROSEXUAL WIRING DIAGRAM
OF TYPICAL MALE
(ON VIAGRA)

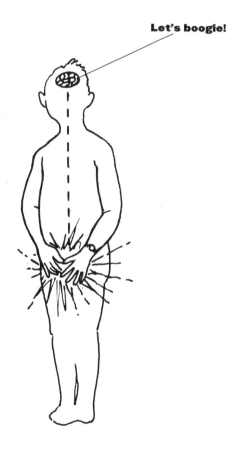

Let's boogie!

HOW MUCH IS TOO MUCH?

Like other powerful drugs, Viagra can lead the unwary or weak-willed into addiction. That's by no means reason to avoid Viagra, but here's a reminder to watch for the warning signals that could mean you need professional help – or at least a night off.

1. Have you been gradually moving your golf, woodworking and other hobbies into bed?   YES ❏   NO ❏

2. When not on Viagra, do you try to recapture that "Viagra feeling" by cutting your veal piccata into diamond shapes?   YES ❏   NO ❏

3. When someone starts telling a Viagra joke, do you unzip your fly and say "*This* is no joke"?   YES ❏   NO ❏

4. When on Viagra, do you regularly ignore your partner's complaints about having a headache? severe spinal injury? the cramped confines of her iron lung?   YES ❏   NO ❏

5. Do you try catching up on your sleep while driving, handling explosives, or working high steel?   YES ❏   NO ❏

If you answered yes to four or more of the above questions, congratulations – you're hooked!

WHAT TO DO IN THE EVENT OF AN OVERDOSE

A bar bet, a tight schedule, a Swedish au pair flying home tomorrow – Viagra binges can happen for lots of reasons. Not to worry when you know these surefire antidotes:

1. Get to a telephone (touch-tone) and speed-dial every woman you know. If this fails,

2. Find a book or set of books on the principles of chartered accountancy and read aloud to yourself until the bed stops spinning. If this fails,

3. Pack your trousers with ice cubes and proceed to the nearest meat locker. If this fails,

4. Draw a picture of Linda Tripp naked. If this fails,

5. Open the bedroom door and have your partner or a friend slam it shut just as you walk through. If this fails,

6. Run hard into a wall, head-on. If this fails,

7. Check to be sure you have actually overdosed on Viagra. The symptoms for the Ebola virus or advanced scurvy can be strikingly similar.

SIDE EFFECTS? NOTHING A LITTLE "VSP" CAN'T CURE!

VSP is a new form of mind control specially developed to help you "keep on truckin'" through those pesky physical discomforts that Viagra use can temporarily trigger.

Briefly put, VSP consists of ensuring mind over matter by training yourself to think one thing while feeling another. It's free, it's fun, it won't cause stomach upset — and it's so simple that presidential candidates have been doing it for years.

Remember: *think one thing while feeling another.*

1. INCREASED PERSPIRATION

The VSP solution: pretend you're a boxer up against Mike Tyson in a fifteen-rounder in Port Said, Egypt. In August. Concentrate! Sweating like a warthog suddenly becomes entirely natural. And besides, you're entitled to pause every three minutes to towel yourself off!

2. BLUISH CAST TO VISION

What a trip, man! Why not VSP yourself all the way back to those psychedelic sixties and the Purple Haze, the Fillmore, free-loving chicks of all creeds and colors? A turn-on! Peace!

Or seize this rare chance to be Picasso in his Blue Period, to see the world as Pablo saw his – minus, of course, the walleyed, squashed-faced women; you're a Viagran, not some cubist nutcake!

One avid PBS watcher uses the mental miracle of VSP to turn his temporarily blue-tinted vision into the wonder of a world seen underwater: a real-life documentary on the Lost City of Atlantis, for example, with himself as Jacques Cousteau.

3. HEADACHES

What's a headache when you're sackbound with Cameron Diaz? If you can VSP your pain into the ecstasy of "making it" with Cameron – or Tia, or Mira, or your high school English teacher – then that relentless pounding, pounding, pounding at the base of your skull is just part of the excitement.

VSP can actually add spice to your love-making. One imaginative Viagran likes to pretend he's just been "caught in the act" by Cameron's jealous boy-friend wielding a ball peen hammer!

In any case, so many other parts of your body will be sending so many messages – most of them pure pleasure – that only a brain hemorrhage could dampen the fun.*

*You'd know it was a brain hemorrhage and not a Viagra side effect if you lose, and never regain, consciousness.

CAVEAT EMPTOR:
ACCEPT NO SUBSTITUTES!

Viagra's overnight success has spawned a pharmaceutical encyclopedia's worth of so-called alternatives that cleverly ape the name but not the efficacy. Be on the alert for:

Vagira

Delivers on its promise of prolonged satisfaction, but how misleading. "Great," grumps one suckered user. "I can now pee for as long as I want."

Most users report feeling "frustrated" by the thirty- to sixty-week wait before Viraga kicks in.

Highly praised for working faster and even more power- fully than Viagra, but a fine-print side effect is its undo- ing: *Warning—May cause irresistible attraction to Canadian waterfowl.*

For constipation, go for it! For sex, no way! Suppository delivery system leaves Varagi DOA.

Exposed almost instantly as a mere placebo, Vigara has nonetheless proven efficacious among its niche market of twelve- to fifteen-year-olds, who throw away the medi- cine and keep the six-pound package full of skin mags it comes wrapped in.

PART II

LIVING WITH VIAGRANS

THE VIAGRASCOPE
WHAT'S YOUR SIGN?

Gone is that humdrum old you, trapped in the funk of sexual insecurity. You're reborn! So chuck all your old astrological charts; they define the universe that *was*. Time to pick your new Sign of the Viagra — and your new destiny along with it!

December 22–January 19 **SUNFISH.**

Your sun's always in the ascendant, and this month it's shining on the house of the rising fun. So how come no Viagra-va-va-voom? Could be that those bikini briefs for a bathing suit, black ankle sox and ghetto blaster are holding back the sand-chicks. But you were born under the sign of the Sunfish, after all, so maximize your potential to be one cool son of the beach. And have a nice day!

January 20–February 18 **PEACOCK.**

Be proud of your prevailing planet and disregard those jokes about your head always being up Uranus. Maybe its powerful pull (in conjunction with Betelgeuse's upcoming sharp left turn at the Crab Nebula) is what's making you overdress. Back off a bit on parading your plumage at the disco come Saturday night. Who knows, maybe this time every last gal won't lock herself in the ladies' room till closing time! And P.S., do up your fly!

February 19–March 20 WILD TURKEY.
Let the Viagra do the talking now that the
house of the seven gables is being ruled by a
dwarf star in transit that controls your libido
and everything else that's not nailed down.
Concentrate this month on clearing your mind of
stinkin' thinkin' and your closet of those old girdle ads.
And remember, you big bad birds were born to party
hearty – but bringing out the whips and chains on a
first date? Whoa!

 March 21–April 19 CRAZY MONKEY.
You're up for anything and everything,
but do be careful for the next few weeks.
Your halfway house will have a direct hit from the twelfth
planet. Meaning? Meaning a Viagra pill could get stuck
in your gullet and give you a stiff neck if you don't play it
as it lays. You may see a stranger across a crowded room:
run to her side, quick as you can, or there'll be blown
fuses all over your solar house.

April 20–May 20 PARTY ANIMAL.
Pigging out on your priapic powers is
going to be tempting. Trouble is, it will
be "that time of the month" for your
would-be conquests, with the moon crossing Main and
Elm just as you hit your favorite fern bar. What to do?
Slip your Viagra supply to a friend and go monastic till it

all blows over. You can use the break to get your leisure suit dry-cleaned, have your teeth fixed and learn to tango. It couldn't hurt!

 **May 21–June 21 LOUNGE LIZARD.** Suave sophisticate of amour, you're going to have spinach in your teeth and stubborn spots on your Dockers this month. Venus will be in a snit from the twenty-second of May to the twentieth of June after finding most stations closed and the twelfth planet in full perigee. Feeling sorry for yourself won't help. Best you can hope for is a date with that beautician with bad breath and hairy arms; if you can penetrate her Baptist restraint, more power to you. You'll need it!

June 22–July 22 STALLION. The retrograde stations of the rulers of your sun are all in seventh heaven this month – and so will you be, *if* you trade in that caveman style for a little TLC.  Bring flowers, candy, and no Black Sabbath CDs. Remember that a pool table is more last resort than first choice; take off your socks; if she won't "talk dirty," lay off the kung fu for once.

 **July 23–August 22 WORM.** You've just done a U-turn that guarantees this worm's going to get his bird, especially now that Mars and your ninth house are on a collision course and the

end of your moon is in sight. But Viagra's not for the meek. Use a hair dryer to warm up those clammy hands if you have to, lose the mason jars and stock your pad with real wineglasses. Decide it's either belt or suspenders but not both. Deep-six the plastic pocket penholder. No more jerking around. Your sexual fate is in your hands!

 August 23–September 22 GOAT. You guys just say *n-a-a-a* to those empty-bedroom blues. No, finesse isn't your bag, and crunching Bud cans with the Bud still in them isn't every woman's idea of a smoothie's how-de-do. But hey, with Neptune banging at the back door of your eleventh house and the solar signs lit up like Times Square for the next few weeks, your rough-and-tumble approach can't miss. And even if it does, well, barnyard animals are no strangers to you frisky critters!

September 23–October 23 DOG. One gander at your planets and it's clear that celibacy is retrograde. Pluto's in your doghouse and Saturn's in your garage just now, you lucky cur. Your only worry is how long the Viagra supply will hold out. So avoid a conniption  and check your prescription. Midway through the month your eighth house may need a roofing job – but if she's the sport we think she is, what's a little thumping and banging between Viagrans?

October 24–November 21 **FOX.**

You sly rascal! There are hens in all
your houses this month, now that
your outer planets are looping the loop and solar
fireworks make turning on the lights redundant. But
you're the kind of guy that makes gals wish there was a
Viagra for attention spans. If you start getting restless,
it's time — for once — to forget the wander and remember
the lust!

November 22–December 21 **BUNNY.**

Quality over quantity: write it on the
inside of your Dr. Dentons. Wham-bam-
thank-you-ma'am may be OK for rabbits,
but it defeats the very purpose of Viagra. So take it slow;
what's the rush, anyway, with your tenth, eleventh and
thirteenth houses on Baltic and Mediterranean and the
night still young? She'll appreciate it, even when you
jump up and get dressed right after, saying you have to
see your insurance man — and it's only 3 a.m.!

VIAGRA AND PETS

Sure, give your dog a bone — but don't push your luck.
Except for their master's leg in the case of larger dog breeds,
male domestic animals need no artificial enhancement to sexual
performance. Just to be safe, Viagra is flavored to taste like dogs to cats
and like cats to dogs. Nonetheless, accidents can happen.

PET	TYPICAL REACTION	WHAT TO DO
Dogs (Especially small breeds such as pugs, Chihuahuas, dachshunds, and bichons frises) 	Exactly the sort of extreme licking, slurping, drooling, snarfing, panting, wheezing, yelping, humping, oozing, piddling behavior you'd expect.	Give him wide berth until his symptoms subside (perhaps go out to a movie). When appropriate, power-hose affected surfaces and rinse with strong veterinary spermicide.
Cats 	Viagra generally has little effect on cats, other than male Abyssinians, who've been known to scrape the wallpaper off the wall after consuming as little as a 50mg tablet.	Consider one of the new Martha Stewart soft-tone paints, especially the corals or clays. They're really quite marvelous.
Mice & Rats 	Even a trace of Viagra sets them off on their treadmills for nonstop sessions lasting as long as 6 to 7 days and nights.	Lubricate wheel with WD-40 or equivalent, as needed.

WHY OLD GOLFERS NEVER DIE

Weekend athletes on Viagra should be aware that carrying added weight in the groin area can cause back problems, strained midsection muscles and hernias – so it's best to wait till you're finished with brisk physical activity and safely home before you "pop one for the lucky ladies."

Golf ranks as the one possible exception. The extra weight and mass are so positioned as to actually encourage a slow, smooth swing and proper tempo without interfering with the clearing of the hips so vital to consistent ball striking. On the other hand, the USGA frowns on the use of Viagra on the links. The ruling is clear: "Carrying an extra club is carrying an extra club."

FINALLY, UGLY IS BEAUTIFUL!

Meet Elle, Cindy and Claudia – no, not *them*, the other Elle, Cindy and Claudia! Physical attributes no longer need be the major criterion for sexual attraction when in the eyes of a Viagran, anything female looks good. What a relief, eh? After all, only insecure men need to chase after supermodels to bolster their own lame sense of sexual self-esteem; and anyway, why should you waste your amazing new powers on some narcissistic dim bulb who can't even spell sex, won't let her hair get mussed, and has stuff in her pocketbook proven to cause brain-cell atrophy and postnasal drip in fashion designers, club owners and laboratory rats?

VIAGRA POWER TOOLS

The fit Viagran is the Viagran best prepared to last longer and finish stronger. But others, such as the elderly and dorks of all ages, are even readier prospects for anything that promises, however marginally, to further "pump them up." Check out the best of athletic and fitness equipment for the active Viagran.

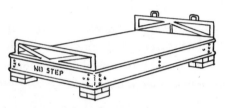

THE VIAGRA HEAVY-DUTY BED

A core of ultrasturdy truck springs under two feet of foam rubber mattress, sandwiched between sheet-metal reinforcing layers for a no-bounce, no-lump ride, and all-welded iron frame and headboard built to WWF standards, combines all-night comfort with an unconditional thirty-year guarantee against sagging and collapse. A permanent asbestos mattress cover and six sets of sweat-repellent sheets are standard.

RUNNING SLIPPERS

High-traction, nonskid, shearling-lined sport slip-ons are specially designed for the bedroom athlete. No more time-wasting slipping and sliding. Kick off in a jiff.

BREAKAWAY PAJAMAS

Why fuss with buttons and drawstrings? Here's snug, stylish nightwear with the warm feel of flannel – but thanks to space-age SmartSeam construction, you're out of your jammies in seconds flat when Aphrodite calls collect!

KING KONGDOMS

The only commercially available condom gorilla-tested for durability in extreme conditions, the meltproof King Kongdom is specially designed for Viagra use. Machine laminated in double-thick miracle Ironhide and triple-vulcanized like a truck tire, but uses "air cushion" technology to make you float like a butterfly, sting like a manta ray.

SELF-DEFENSE FOR WOMEN IN THE VIAGRA AGE

You're perched at the bar, hoping for some Friday night happy hour social action, when the guy bursts through the door without using his hands.

"Hey, you," he coos. "Wanna see me bore another hole in the wall in this hole-in-the-wall?"

Some pickup line! "Get lost, creep" might be your normal comeback. But realize it could be the Viagra talking, and cut him some slack. After all, he's suddenly got blood rushing to places not even shown in *Gray's Anatomy,* and it's making him giddy. That oh-so-casual way of saying hello just could be your introduction to Mister Thrills 'n' Chills. Moral: get to know the guy behind the bluster before you brush him off.

But before anything else, make sure he's a real Viagran and not one of the many impostors trying to "pass" without paying their $10 per pill or supercharging their manhood.

Check first for drool. Viagrans generally run a loose mouth but a dry one; if the saliva doesn't stop dripping off his chin after half an hour or so, you're probably bantering with what experts call a mongolian idiot.

Next, ask him the pharmaceutical name for Viagra. He'll shoot back "Sildenafil citrate" — or you're playing footsie with a phony. Real Viagrans read their prescription labels like Warren Buffett reads the NASDAQ board, to avoid prepping for a night of joy by accidentally downing Flintstones vitamins or a worming agent.

Okay, the guy's kosher. But is he a mensch or a menace?

Here's a foolproof test: knee him in the groin. If he doubles over cursing and stumbles out of the bar, it proves he was after only one thing. But if he turns away to quietly regurgitate and then cracks something witty about the "family jewels," babe, you've picked yourself a gem!

Additional Viagra alerts:

◆ As the big Viagra Moment draws near, chances are he'll be too "hot to trot" to practice the niceties. So steer him gently in the right direction. "Do you always walk on your knees?" "You'll be comfier with your shoes off." "That's the pillow, I'm over here." Remember, the male ego is so fragile. Scolding might break the mood.

◆ Never leave liver, a catcher's mitt or other receptacle lying around the bedroom when you're with a Viagran. *And don't leave the bedroom.* Viagrans simply hate to wait; you could return from powdering your nose to confront a horrifying tableau.

The rules for dating a Viagran are basically simple. One, let him make the first move. This should normally come just after "hello" but before you can put on your hat. If it doesn't, you have the right to ask if he's been with someone else since he got on the elevator. Two, keep track of time. Be sure your cats are fed for the next few days and that the cable TV bill is paid in advance.

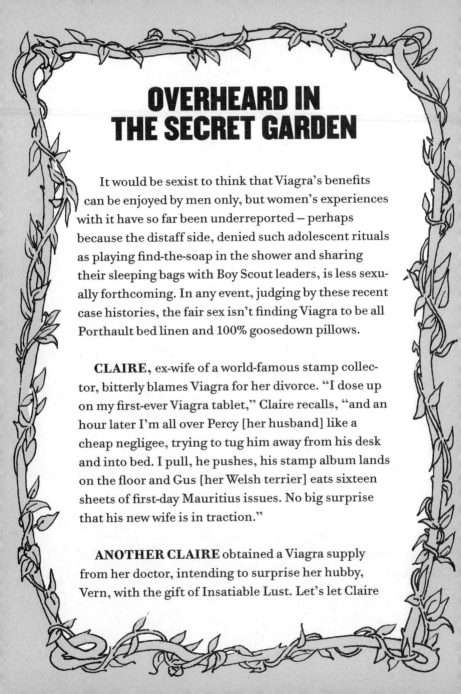

OVERHEARD IN THE SECRET GARDEN

It would be sexist to think that Viagra's benefits can be enjoyed by men only, but women's experiences with it have so far been underreported — perhaps because the distaff side, denied such adolescent rituals as playing find-the-soap in the shower and sharing their sleeping bags with Boy Scout leaders, is less sexually forthcoming. In any event, judging by these recent case histories, the fair sex isn't finding Viagra to be all Porthault bed linen and 100% goosedown pillows.

CLAIRE, ex-wife of a world-famous stamp collector, bitterly blames Viagra for her divorce. "I dose up on my first-ever Viagra tablet," Claire recalls, "and an hour later I'm all over Percy [her husband] like a cheap negligee, trying to tug him away from his desk and into bed. I pull, he pushes, his stamp album lands on the floor and Gus [her Welsh terrier] eats sixteen sheets of first-day Mauritius issues. No big surprise that his new wife is in traction."

ANOTHER CLAIRE obtained a Viagra supply from her doctor, intending to surprise her hubby, Vern, with the gift of Insatiable Lust. Let's let Claire

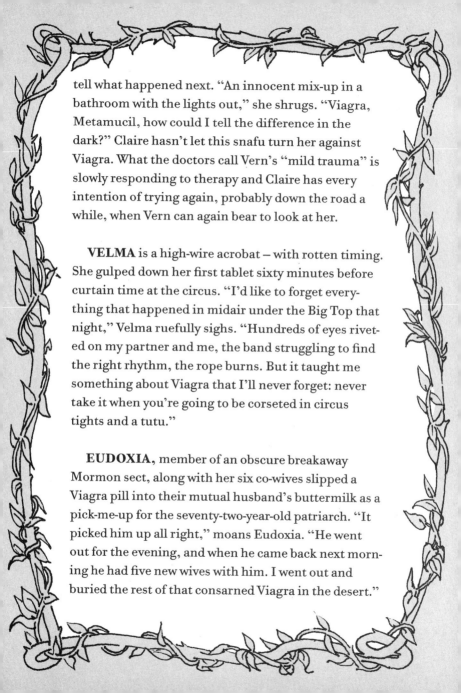

tell what happened next. "An innocent mix-up in a bathroom with the lights out," she shrugs. "Viagra, Metamucil, how could I tell the difference in the dark?" Claire hasn't let this snafu turn her against Viagra. What the doctors call Vern's "mild trauma" is slowly responding to therapy and Claire has every intention of trying again, probably down the road a while, when Vern can again bear to look at her.

VELMA is a high-wire acrobat — with rotten timing. She gulped down her first tablet sixty minutes before curtain time at the circus. "I'd like to forget everything that happened in midair under the Big Top that night," Velma ruefully sighs. "Hundreds of eyes riveted on my partner and me, the band struggling to find the right rhythm, the rope burns. But it taught me something about Viagra that I'll never forget: never take it when you're going to be corseted in circus tights and a tutu."

EUDOXIA, member of an obscure breakaway Mormon sect, along with her six co-wives slipped a Viagra pill into their mutual husband's buttermilk as a pick-me-up for the seventy-two-year-old patriarch. "It picked him up all right," moans Eudoxia. "He went out for the evening, and when he came back next morning he had five new wives with him. I went out and buried the rest of that consarned Viagra in the desert."

LADIES: IN THE AGE OF VIAGRA, WHO TURNS YOU ON?

Find out in this fun quiz! Just match the proven
"turn-on" word on this page with the profession opposite.
Remember, there are no wrong answers!

Backdraft

Rubdown

Gallon of skim

Stirrups

Rainer Maria Rilke

Aye, yer a spitfire!

God is love!

Rape fantasies

Hey lady, nice tits!

Touché!

My fellow Americans

Dig it, man

Masseur

Milkman

Gynecologist

Pirate

Evangelist

**English
Professor**

Fireman

Fencer

Psychiatrist

**L.A. Coffeehouse
Musician**

**Construction
Worker**

U.S. President

MALE COUPLING DEVICE IDENTI-CHART

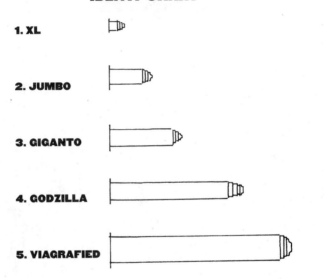

1. XL

2. JUMBO

3. GIGANTO

4. GODZILLA

5. VIAGRAFIED

Note: Female nomenclature for male coupling devices is different: 1. = OK; 2. = Cute; 3. = Sweet; 4. = Darling; 5. = My Great Big Naughty Boy.

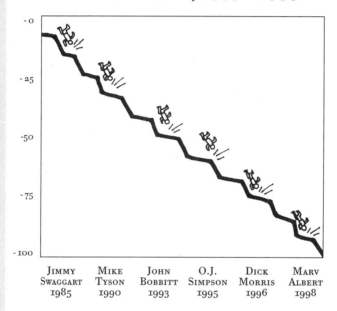

SEXUAL APPEAL OF THE AMERICAN MALE, 1985 – 1998

| JIMMY SWAGGART 1985 | MIKE TYSON 1990 | JOHN BOBBITT 1993 | O.J. SIMPSON 1995 | DICK MORRIS 1996 | MARV ALBERT 1998 |

The above chart may help explain the current popularity of Ellen DeGeneres. Further erosion of male sexual appeal is expected when a broader study, which will include Bruce Willis, Dennis Rodman and Yanni, is concluded.

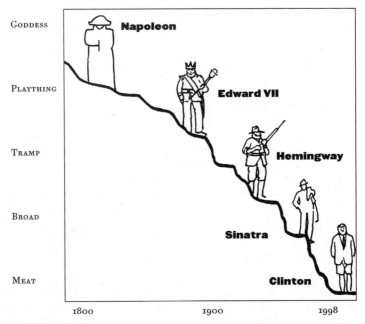

RESPECT FOR WOMEN AMONG MALES 40 TO 60 YEARS (1800-1998)

GODDESS — Napoleon

PLAYTHING — Edward VII

TRAMP — Hemingway

BROAD — Sinatra

MEAT — Clinton

1800   1900   1998

Given their role models over time, it's hardly surprising that men's respect for women has plummeted since 1800. Anxious sexologists are pinning their hopes for a future reversal on Leonardo DiCaprio, though it may take a couple of decades before he fully matures.

THE MALE VIAGRAN'S GUIDE TO THE INNER WORLD OF WOMEN

You may think you know what makes the fair sex tick (and tickle!), but check recent surveys: only one man in ten knows how earrings work. Fewer than one in twenty can name the thirty-two commonest items found in a woman's handbag. Four in ten men believe "menopause" is a warning for them to slow down on the highway. The truth is, such ignorance can lead to blunders serious enough to blunt the charge of a 350-pound Viagran in heat. Study and memorize these key facts. The Viagra Moment you save may be your own!

HANDBAG A striking manifestation of the female collecting instinct. Women derive deep emotional security from keeping these portable receptacles, packed with what we would call "junk" and often weighing several pounds, close by at all times – to the point of lugging them, in groups, to the ladies' room to compare treasures. Don't sneer. That "junk" – Kleenex balls, empty Evian bottles, multiple pairs of sunglasses, Dutch coins, Rolodex cards, cell phone, fabric samples ad infinitum – is to them what a blanket is to Linus.

LINGERIE An amazing number of well-intentioned men purchase expensive and often erotically stimulating undergarments as gifts for women even though they know from observation that women actually wear simple, practical cotton. C'mon, fellas! Women find slinky lingerie a turnoff — but they just can't get enough free junk-mail lingerie catalogs! So forget the French satin and Chantilly lace: Just dump a pile of Victoria's Secret catalogs in her lap. And watch her light up!

MEDICINE CHEST A stationary receptacle for one or another particular female collectible, e.g., empty bottles, jars and boxes; forgotten or failed cosmetic experiments; discarded tooth- and hairbrushes; hair. NOTE: NEVER ATTEMPT TO REORGA-NIZE! That seemingly haphazard assemblage represents an intricate and interlinked system of superstitions and beliefs that lie at the very core of womanhood. To disturb it is to court disaster — as in, "No nooky for you, Mister Man!"

KLEENEX BALLS It's all too typical of male smugness that few men have ever bothered to find out why these exist in such astounding numbers. Nose wiping and lipstick erasing are secondary reasons. Women stuff their purses with Kleenex balls because they're impelled by their fierce instinct for survival: if snatched by terrorists, the cool-witted feminine captive can leave behind a telltale trail of fluffy little signposts that will lead the cops  straight to the rebels' lair! No wonder reports of women being whisked off to Libya are so rare.

EMERY BOARDS Not the old popsicle sticks they seem, but in fact a modern-day version of old-fashioned worry beads. Women use emery boards to soothe low-grade anxiety with small, regular, harmless rubbing action on their nails during conversation or TV watching.

Caution: A woman's use of an emery board during sex may be a sign that your Viagra pill isn't working.

THE TELLTALE SIGNS OF VIAGRAPHOBIA

Ignorant, superstitious, jealous, petty and hobbled by narrow religious beliefs – don't let these flaws mask the fact that people hate you most of all because you're a Viagran: proud and ready to go at all times.

Only a very few will dare express their antipathy to your face. Viagraphobia is sly and sinister, all winks and gestures and awkward silences – like marriage, if not quite so hostile. Typical Viagraphobe behavior to watch for:

- They blush beet-red whenever the conversation turns to mailing tubes.

- They won't let their kiddies sit in your lap.

- They will dance with you only at the other end of a twelve-foot extension cord.

- They introduce you to their friends by sticking out their tongues, rolling their eyes and making rapid right-hand stroking motions.

- They lock up canine females in estrus when you visit.

◆ They hide the tub of I Can't Believe It's Not Butter if you're staying overnight and didn't bring a date.

◆ They give you nitroglycerin as a birthday gift.

◆ They claim not to have any Barry White records — even if you never asked.

Remember, discrimination of any kind should not be tolerated. If you believe yourself to be the victim of Viagraphobia, prepare a brief and send it to:

U.S. Supreme Court
Washington, D.C.
ATTN: Justice Clarence Thomas

Rx FOR FOOLING
MR. PHARMACIST

Want it noised around town that you need extra lead in your pencil? Of course not. Here's a quartet of tricks to throw the pharmacist off the scent next time you need your prescription filled:

1) Rent the room above the pharmacy, cut a hole in the floor, and lower your Rx on a string with a note saying you're really Howard Hughes and there's $1 million in it for hush-hush service.

2) Wear a Nixon mask and tell the pharmacist you aren't dead but were kidnapped on your 1972 China visit on orders from J. Edgar Hoover—and now that you're back home at last, have just got to try this new Viagra thing.

3) Find a pair of identical twins who look just like you, then all three pay Mr. Pharmacist a visit, saying (in unison), "I'd like this prescription filled, please." Three of you and one prescription; he'll be flummoxed but good!

4) Drop by your local anarchist supply house en route to the drugstore and pick up a medium-sized throwing bomb with AAA-length wick. Plunk the bomb, wick lit, on the counter and count to five. As soon as the pharmacist has fled, douse the wick and go grab all the Viagra you want.

FASHION PREVIEW:
THE VIAGRA LOOK

**Cock o' the Walk
Casuals**

**Viagra pride? He can't
keep it down!**

**Dennis is up for
tennis . . .**

**Can you say
"fore" play?**

**. . . and these togs fit
this Dick to a tee.**

**Businesswear bulges
with authority**

HOME SWEET NURSING HOME

Viagra's advent has in one sudden gust of chemical energy swept aside the checkers games, Lawrence Welk reruns and the Depends fights that were their nearest thing to fun, granting the roosters among our golden-oldster flock an encore run at the henhouse.

The traditional American nursing or "rest" home will soon be obsolete. Rest? No rest for the wicked – not for that wicked ol' devil who's just exchanged his custard-stained hospital gown and saline drip for glad rags and some salty happy hour banter with the buxom widow lady down the hall. Not for the Viagra-popping grandpop who may not always remember who he is but who's definitely forgotten boredom.

Reborn senior rakehells should use common sense, of course: understanding how a paternity suit can mangle a fixed income; grasping the potential legal downside to asking the night nurse if you can sponge-bathe *her* this time.

But let's give that crusty Casanova a little credit for the smarts that come from romantic experience. After all, the guy's been around the bed a few times before. Remember, he's still a wise old owl – just a hornier one!

THE SENIOR SUTRA

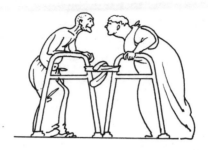

Confinement to a walker should not keep Viagra-phile seniors from "getting it on" in their golden years. Just follow the "Three P's" – Prudence, Preparation and Pauses for Breath – and these precise instructions.

THE FRENCH BEND Facing each other, shuffle walkers forward until they meet with no space between. The man joins walkers together by tying belt of his bathrobe around the front upper horizontal or vertical bars of both devices, checking for a tight fit by shaking. The two walkers should now feel like one. With both of you firmly gripping walker bars, you can commence pursuit of your Viagra Moment.

THE HINDU TWIST If fatigue should set in after you have maintained a standing position for several minutes but both partners are in reasonable physical condition (no broken bones), grasp each other firmly about the waist and lean to the right until walkers, and you, topple over. You are now lying in the desired horizontal position. When you have "finished your business," ask an attendant or close relative to right the walkers and you. Untie the bathrobe belt and shuffle slowly back to your quarters.

CRUTCH CAPERS Easy as pie! Would-be partners hobble to opposite sides of the bed, throw down their crutches and commence La Vie Viagra.

Caution: always throw crutches to the side or behind you. One overeager couple at a Louisville nursing home flung theirs so heedlessly that they knocked each other out. When they regained consciousness, mutual lust had turned to such mutual anger that this time the crutches flew in earnest and they knocked each other out again – and neither has spoken an intelligible word since!

THE AUSTRIAN FLOP It's not the most exciting, but it's definitely the safest solution. Have someone place a mattress on the floor between your two wheelchairs. Then carefully – carefully, now! – lean forward and fall onto it. Be sure not to knock heads; there are no His & Hers suites in most brain surgery units.

PART III

IT'S A VIAGRA WORLD

VIAGRAMART

A CATALOG OF PERSONAL ACCESSORIES
TO ENHANCE THE VIAGRA LIFESTYLE

Lo-Rider Cummerbund

This elegant wrap-around satin-finish garment is the perfect way to painlessly quell an unwelcome Viagra uprising at bar mitzvahs, diplomatic receptions, debutante balls – or to be prepared beforehand, just in case.

Glo-in-the-Dark Bedpost Viagra Dispenser ends those exhausting 3 a.m. trips to the medicine chest when light-sleeping seniors find themselves "hot to trot." Loading's a snap – and when supply runs low an electronic voice automatically advises, "Time to refill!" in fluent Korean.

"Sinking Liner" Pool Caddy snaps onto any bathing suit in seconds when the Viagra kicks in, turning those "awkward moments" into fun conversation while stumping the kiddies. (Specify Titanic, Lusitania or Andrea Doria)

Lawrence Welk Moving Eyes Bedside Table Romance Center

Keep your honey "in the Viagra Zone" with this CD player that looks like a handsomely framed portrait. Romance is in the air as that "Champagne Music" oozes from hidden stereo speakers – and Lawrence himself seems to be following and encouraging her every love move.

Party Propeller Caught in "Viagra fla-grante" at a gala social event? The Party Propeller makes a madcap offense the best defense! Starts spinning the instant you slip it on over your pants and cinch the size-adjustable "comfort ring" – and you're off, racing around the room playing airplane! Startled friends are too busy laugh-ing with you to laugh at you; sixty-second power burst is enough to get you safely to the bath-room before the crowd wises up.

Telescopic Fishing Pole Extension Outdoor sportsmen rave about its hands-off convenience, even when not experienc-ing the "Viagra effect."

SENIORS SPECIALS VIAGRAMART

"Viagra Nights" Glamour Gown wears like a hospital gown, ties at the back in a jiff, but looks like a tux to spice up those special heavy dates. Includes set of six separate dickeylike spittle bibs.

Pocket Swiss Army Viagralarm sounds rousing "Ride of the Valkyries" music theme sixty minutes after he takes his Viagra, to remind the forgetful senior that "it's time to rumble."

One-Size-Fits-All Elbow Guards, molded in soft and pliable Geriatra, protect Viagra-inspired senior "love machine's" sensitive elbow skin from chafing, sheet burns, etc.

Energy-saving "Orgasmatic 2000" Beeper sounds when you've finished your "whoopee." No wondering, no waiting. No itchy wires, no heavy batteries.

Lifelike 100% Genuine Vinyl Hollywood Star Face Mask hides your partner's wrinkles, wattles, nose hair, etc., to take your lovemaking back fifty, sixty years or more. Eye, nose and mouth holes for wearer comfort. (Specify Louise Brooks, Mary Pickford, Sylvia Miles)

"Sheik of Araby" Deluxe Oxygen Tent Inside tent walls printed with romantic palm-tree-and-camel motif. Comes with furlike 4×4-foot rug, six throw pillows, monogrammed palm-frond hand fan with built-in emergency buzzer. ER-approved design makes a love nest of an urgent medical necessity!

VIAGRA RESHAPES OUR WORLD

The unique Viagra lifestyle penetrates every nook and cranny of society. After learning that even with Viagra, men are still too afraid of her to make advances, Martha Stewart sells her magazine and becomes coach of the Dallas Cowboys. The magazine reappears as *Viagra Living* and becomes financially engorged.

Detroit redefines driving comfort for the American male, just in time to stop a rash of accidents caused by loss of steering control.

Swank restaurants put new emphasis on catering to their patrons' individual needs.

"One more time, Pop. Which one's the Viagra, and which is the suppository?"

NASA must spend $1.8 billion to redesign astronauts' flight suits after Viagrans' Rights Bill passes Senate.

To placate Viagra users – and limit damage to seats – the Metropolitan Opera announces a fifty-nine-minute production of Wagner's *Tristan und Isolde.*

AREAS OF HIGHEST VIAGRA PENETRATION IN THE U.S.

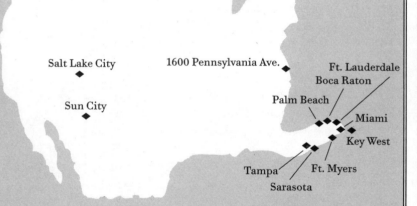

Salt Lake City

1600 Pennsylvania Ave.

Sun City

Ft. Lauderdale
Boca Raton
Palm Beach
Miami
Key West
Tampa
Ft. Myers
Sarasota

AREAS OF LOWEST VIAGRA PENETRATION IN THE U.S.

VIAGRA TOURIST TREASURES & TRAPS

WORTH A VISIT

VIAGRATRAZ, San Francisco, California. As befits America's only Viagra-themed amuse-

ment park, Viagratraz is sited beyond the reach of the underaged in a converted federal prison facility on a rock in San Francisco Bay. Its adults-only attractions include the Sperm Race thrill ride, the Love Tunnel (spooky!), the Mammary Mountain roller coaster, and a slippery climb up Captain Dick's Pillar to the revolving Hard Rocks Cafe.

MUST-MISSES

VIAGRA WAX MUSEUM, Hollywood, California. Errol Flynn, Warren Beatty, Charlton Heston, Fatty Arbuckle and forty-two other immortal Tinseltown ladykillers as lifelike wax mannequins, purporting to show how each would have looked sixty minutes after taking Viagra. Alas, temperatures in this tiny lair often hit 100°F, and all that melting wax defeats the sense of realism, not to mention the drama.

VIAGRA VILLAGE, Sturbridge, Massachusetts. A creative but misguided off-shoot of the Viagra phenomenon: folk dressed in eighteenth-century colonial garb handcrafting tasteless giant vibrating candles, crocheting on distinctly phallic throw pillows bearing such lamely comic mottos as "Don't Tread On Me" and baking "Viagra cakes" allegedly based on a recipe invented by Jenny McCarthy. Not for the squeamish – or the kiddies.

NATURAL BIDET, Petrified Corners, Arizona. French tourists appear to shrug off the $10 admission and twelve-mile walk through rattlesnake country to view this freak of

geology, but even diehard Viagrans may wish to skip it – especially when Navajo snakeskin condoms are for sale (at bargain prices) just 378 miles farther along Highway 50.

SUCKLEY'S BED & BREAKFAST, Ashfield, Massachusetts. For your $5, Mrs. Suckley will allow a peep into the upstairs back bedroom where Viagra was allegedly first used one Friday night in 1992 by two pharmaceutical lab researchers in an unauthorized experiment. Five-dollar surcharge if you upset Mrs. Suckley's three miniature poodles.

VIAGRA ARTS & CRAFTS

Viagra has so quickly seeped deep into the lives of average Americans that folk arts and crafts are already reflecting its influence. Why not stage your own Viagra Fair, Festival or Bee? All you need is yarn, macramé, old coat hangers, a few pounds of carrot bread and the use of a Grange Hall — and pretty soon, your local paper could be publishing something like this:

Mrs. Winnifred Beasley's *Winged Viagra* took First Prize in the Jell-O Sculpture category at the Viagra Folk Arts & Crafts Council's first annual Viagraboree, with all proceeds going to buy mattresses for the needy. (Are you listening, Ace Greenberg?)

Mr. Wilf Beasley walked off with a Best in Show, Knickknacks category, for his *Lawn Jockey on Viagra* driftwood-and-sausage construction. The quilting bee produced a colorful king-sized reversible coverlet with a floral bouquet on one side and beautifully needlepointed scenes from *Debbie Does Dallas* on the reverse. A demonstration of how to strip a bed with someone still in it had to be suspended when someone else got in, but the Viagradance contest attracted couples of all ages.

The Viagratones band under the twin batons (actually drumsticks!) of leader Sid Beasley was back by popular demand — back in a far corner — and once again closed out festivities at the Viagra Arts & Crafts Viagraboree  with their theme song, "I'm in the Mood for Love." The V-Tones played straight through to the wee hours, even though the Viagraboree was over at 6:30 p.m.

 The evening's door prize, an exotic nude oil painting titled *Winnie Don't I Wish*, signed Fliw Yelsaeb, was won by Mr. and Mrs. W. Beasley. Beasley Pharmacy, your friendly and reliable stop for all your prescription, personal care and adult video needs.

VIAGRA NATION'S MODEL

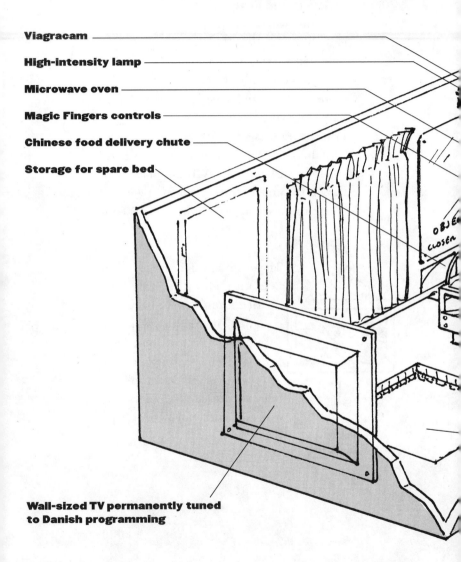

Viagracam

High-intensity lamp

Microwave oven

Magic Fingers controls

Chinese food delivery chute

Storage for spare bed

OBJE
CLOSE

Wall-sized TV permanently tuned
to Danish programming

BEDROOM OF TOMORROW

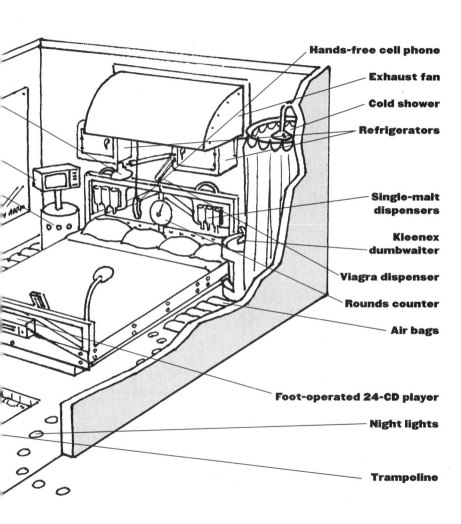

Hands-free cell phone

Exhaust fan

Cold shower

Refrigerators

Single-malt dispensers

Kleenex dumbwaiter

Viagra dispenser

Rounds counter

Air bags

Foot-operated 24-CD player

Night lights

Trampoline

VIAGRA COMMEMORATIVES
WHY NOT BEGIN YOUR OWN ALBUM TODAY?

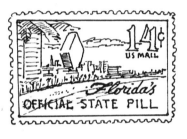

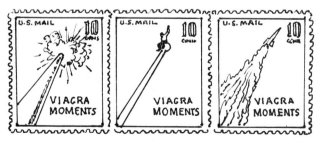

POSTCARDS FROM VIAGRALAND

HI!   THURSDAY

VISITED THE NEW VIAGRA FALLS
HONEYMOON RESORT NEAR INTERCOURSE,
PA. WOW! THEY SAY IT'S
GIVEN THE LOCAL ECONOMY A
REAL SPURT! STRANGEST SIGHT
ON THE TRIP — ALL THOSE
THRUSTING MARBLE SHAFTS! THEY
SAY "WASHINGTON MONUMENT
SYNDROME" HIT LANDMARK
ARCHITECTS LIKE THE FLU RIGHT
AFTER VIAGRA CAME OUT.
COINCIDENCE? AND HOW ABOUT
THE ERECT TOWER OF PISA?
VIAGRA ANNOUNCED, NEXT DAY IT
STRAIGHTENS ITSELF RIGHT OUT! THE
WHOLE WORLD'S BECOMING ONE BIG
VIAGRA NATION!!!

VIAGRALAND
PM
16 JUN
1998

POST CARD

25

VIAGRA FALLS

MR + MRS VICTOR VIAGRA
28 VIAGRA WAY
VIAGRAVILLE, VA
V.S.A.

FIRST CLASS

— LOVE FROM MARCEL

Greetings from Viagra Falls

THE VIAGRA MEDIA EXPLOSION

Are the media making too much of Viagra, or what? Here's a random sampling of what's currently playing down at the corner newsstand.

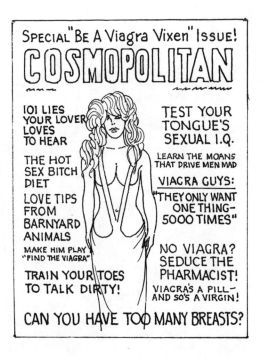

SPECIAL "BE A Viagra Vixen" ISSUE!

COSMOPOLITAN

101 LIES YOUR LOVER LOVES TO HEAR

THE HOT SEX BITCH DIET

LOVE TIPS FROM BARNYARD ANIMALS

MAKE HIM PLAY "FIND THE VIAGRA"

TRAIN YOUR TOES TO TALK DIRTY!

TEST YOUR TONGUE'S SEXUAL I.Q.

LEARN THE MOANS THAT DRIVE MEN MAD

VIAGRA GUYS: "THEY ONLY WANT ONE THING— 5000 TIMES"

NO VIAGRA? SEDUCE THE PHARMACIST!

VIAGRA'S A PILL— AND SO'S A VIRGIN!

CAN YOU HAVE TOO MANY BREASTS?

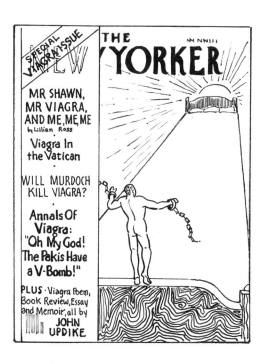

RollingStone

HUNTER S. THOMPSON'S VIAGRA ORGY
An Almost Complete Sentence

THE ROLLING STONE HEADLINE:
COURTNEY LOVE, MEL GIBSON,
VIAGRA, MICK, THE RAIN FOREST

Rolling Stone's 1999 Viagra OD Preview
Rolling Stone's 1998 Viagra OD Review

THE ROLLING STONE INTERVIEW:
Courtney Love's Not Talking

The Rolling Stone Exclusive:
Hanson Takes Viagra,
Explodes: Will the Tour
Go On?

THE ROLLING STONE
QUESTION:
HOW UNHIP IS VIAGRA?

ROLLING STONE'S
P.J. O'ROURKE'S
WEIRD BAREFOOT VIAGRA
QUEST FOR SASQUATCH

VANITY FAIR

CAN VIAGRA
RAISE THE
DEAD MAFIA
EUROTRASH?

PALM BEACH STORY:
THE DEAD EX- NAZI
SWINDLER AND THE
HOLLYWOOD VIAGRA
MAFIOSO

THE BILLION-
DOLLAR
EURONAZI-
HEIRESS VIAGRA
STOCK SWINDLE

VIAGRA PUNKS:
PALM BEACH'S
NEW EUROMAFIA

HOLLYWOOD
EUROPUNKS
IN VIAGRA HEAVEN

AN ANNIE LIEBOWITZ PORTFOLIO

MAFIA SUPERMODELS WHO
SWAP NAZI PUNKS FOR VIAGRA

THE VIAGRA BOOKSHELF
TOPPING THE BEST-SELLER LIST

**DON'T SWEAT THE SEX STUFF, AND IT'S ALL
SEX STUFF** Advice and how-to tips on lovemaking
delivered in a jaunty, happy-go-lucky style: "Stop blub-
bering! Your partner's sudden death during sex can do
wonders for your self-esteem!"

**EVERYTHING I KNOW ABOUT SEX I LEARNED
SECONDHAND** All redheads are nymphomaniacs;
syphilis breeds on toilet seats; masturbation causes
homosexuality – and a hundred more astonishing sexual
revelations.

THE VIAGRA CONSPIRACY – HOAX OR PLOT?
How the CIA and the Freemasons co-developed Viagra to
distract American males so they won't notice the alien
spacecraft landings that signal step one in the Trilateral
Commission's takeover of the world.

THE 30-SECOND VIAGRAN Streamlined techniques
for busy managers. Why Unzip?; Bye-Bye Beds; E-Mail
Pillowtalk; Fax As You F——; and fifty-two other time and
energy-saving drills. Reading time: 10 min. 30 secs.

VIAGRAN FROM NAZARETH Inspiration and sacri-
lege compete as a biblical scholar interprets the Old

Testament to prove that Moses engraved the Ten Commandments on Viagra tablets to test the faith of his people – and how it nearly backfired.

TRY THE SOFA CUSHIONS Hilarious tales from the Viagra Age by one of our foremost humorist/philosopher/moralist/MC/song-and-dance men, whose homey anecdotes always leave you undecided whether to laugh, take a bath or go to church (not necessarily in that order).

RED SUN OVER VIAGRA Soaring birthrate, plummeting workplace productivity, a nation gone soft with pleasure seeking – how America's Viagra obsession plays into the hands of Japan's Central Bank and ensures that we will all be their houseboys by 2010.

THE VIAGRAN NEXT DOOR Peeking in his window, miking his bed, hiding in his bedroom closet – studying, really studying the ways of the Viagran next door can lead to much more than just a nasty harassment lawsuit.

. . . AND I'LL LIVE TO BE A HUNDRED These posthumous memoirs of a self-confessed "Viagra addict," obscenity-laced and off-puttingly repetitive, are alternately boastful ("She offered me her Buick if I'd give her five more minutes") and self-pitying ("It was only a lousy Skylark"), but never less than incoherent. An Editors' Choice.

VIAGRAMAN KOMIX

The awesomely endowed "Caped Codpiece" is sworn to use his manly weaponry only in the cause of world peace, environmental safety, animal rights and good hot sex between consenting adults. Never shown naked or in full-frontal or profile view, Viagraman nonetheless is seen performing astonishing feats of strength and derring-do without the aid of hands or feet.

The climax of every Viagraman strip is a confrontation with a bluenose, hypocrite or do-gooder. Not shown here: Viagraman's concern for the healthy sexual development of America's youth. Indeed, the strip titled "Billy in the Bathroom," with Viagraman's outburst in the penultimate panel ("Dammit, Billy, you're shaking the place apart!!!") won the 1998 Decency in Culture for Kids Golden Dick.

INTRODUCING
THE 1999 CADILLAC VIAGRA

With its exclusive Magic Fingers Ride, trunk-mounted shower and daringly innovative "Backseat Driver" steering technology, Cadillac's new special-edition Viagra model looks to be just the ticket for a Viagra Nation on the move.

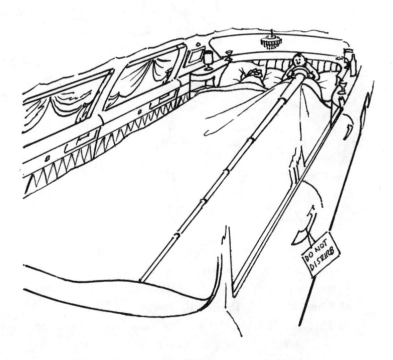

VIAGRA: WHAT'S IN, WHAT'S OUT

IN	OUT
Amy Fisher	Lorena Bobbitt
Hard drives	Floppies
Intercourse, PA	Blue Ball, PA
The Hardy Boys	Ragged Dick
Rigid airships	Balloons
Cucumbers	Baby carrots
The pole vault	Sprints
The Magnificent Seven	*Twelve Angry Men*
The Little Engine That Could	Pat the Bunny
Good Humor	Mister Softee
The whole nine yards	A game of inches
Knockwurst	Cocktail franks
Big Bertha	Little Nell

WHO SAID WHAT IN VIAGRA NATION THIS YEAR?

TEST YOUR VQ! NOW!

1. Erica Jong, author
2. Elizabeth Dole, Bob's babe
3. Irving Mesher, seventy-three-year-old retiree, nudist camp resident
4. Susie Bright, on-line columnist, www.salon1999.com
5. Gail Sheehy, passagist
6. John W. Weigel, M.D., urologist
7. Maureen Dowd, *New York Times* punditrix
8. David Letterman, late-night TV host

a. "I have sex three or four times a week with girl-friends in their twenties."
b. "My face got flushed."
c. "It allows [sexual performance] to be talked about at the breakfast table."
d. "My arm is getting tired."
e. "Ellen DeGeneres and Anne Heche will announce they want to have a baby. Man, that Viagra's really something."
f. "You guys can't have it if we can't have fen-phen."
g. "He was in the protocol. It's a great drug!"
h. "Raises the Dow and the penis, too."

Answers: 1-h; 2-g; 3-a; 4-b; 5-c; 6-d; 7-f; 8-e

"REAL MEN DON'T NEED VIAGRA"
A CRY FOR HELP

"Norman," a semiretired amateur boxer, protested vehemently that "real men don't need Viagra" when the miracle drug first appeared — a mite too vehemently, top specialists suspected.

Sure enough, Norman's machomaniacal outbursts turned out to be a symptom of a rare neurological disorder, combining elements of Tourette's syndrome and coprolalia, known as Mailer's Disease and probably caused by too many blows to an already distended ego.

Only one in every hundred or so sentences uttered by a person suffering from Mailer's Disease makes sense, yet the victim is compelled to utter more and more sentences. There is no miracle drug in the offing that promises even partial recovery. Meanwhile, Norm has at least learned to medicate himself by venting his rage on paper, a harmless pastime that keeps him off the streets and out of trouble.

E PLURIBUS SILDENAFIL

Our federal government is already responding to the Viagra Age, in diverse ways. Herewith a roundup of top stories from Viagra Nation's capital.

◆ The Senate votes next month on a bill establishing a Cabinet-level Department of Viagrification, to keep the president personally up-to-date on sexual potency research and research interns.

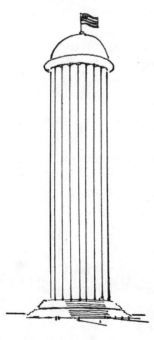

◆ The federal Drug Enforcement Agency has already failed to intercept $1 billion per day of illegal Viagra shipments and has asked Mexico to keep the noise down at night.

◆ Construction of a Tomb of the Unknown Viagran has been approved by the Senate in memory of those anonymous men in black socks and masks who gave their all – and a fatal push more – in the clinical trials that led to the introduction of Viagra.

Tomb of the Unknown Viagran

Brazilian rain forest before (left) and after (right) Viagra dusting

◆ Formation of a National Viagra Party, calling for Viagra to be pulverized and sprayed over the Brazilian rain forest to make the trees stand tall and proud, has been announced by former California governor Jerry Brown, who intends to run for president in 2000 on a platform of burning coals and nails.

◆ Congress will shortly pass a resolution establishing the last Sunday in August as Viagra Day, when adult Americans will be encouraged to remain in bed for twenty-four hours. The date was

First Viagra Day parade found everybody home in bed watching it on TV

carefully chosen. On the last Sunday in August, a) TV is showing nothing but reruns anyway, b) the kids are playing outdoors, c) partners will both have summer tans and look gorgeous.

VIAGRA'S FORGOTTEN VICTIMS

It would be wrong to suggest that Viagra has been champagne and roses for everybody. Average Americans just like you are turned into gutter scum daily by Viagra overuse and abuse. Consider these three case histories, and let them be a lesson to us all.

1) Pepperdine University's 1987 "Mr. Pep," Tommy tried Viagra "on a dare" and had soon sold his college sweetheart into white slavery to support his twenty-times-a-day sex habit. Money long since gone, Tommy's now desperately panhandling to finance a last-chance sex-change operation.

2) Milt skipped bowling one night for a Hollywood orgy and somebody slipped a Viagra into his Mai Tai. Presto: the stud of Tinseltown . . . until Viagra Burn-out. Too weak to leave his flophouse bed, Milt talks of marketing a four-foot "Viagrasicle" and wonders aloud where all the gals have gone.

3) High-born Freddie thought his bachelor's Viagra honeymoon would never end. Then the trysts and weekend invitations dwindled. Finally, the doctors broke the tragic news: Freddie had worn himself down to – literally – a nub. He's sold his penthouse and will soon be off to a Saudi Arabian palace and a new career as an in-house castrato.

WAS IT GOOD FOR YOU?

GOOD VIAGRA CITIZENSHIP

With power comes responsibility.

The wise Viagran remembers this, and takes special care not to trample the freedoms and rights of others.

Cut out this list of no-no's and carry it in your wallet, paste it inside your fedora or hang it off your fly zipper as a handy reference.

DON'T – even in jest – disport in public claiming that "I'm a policeman and this is my billy club!" Impersonating a law officer often means heavy fines.

DON'T try amusing your date in a fine restaurant by grabbing lettuce from her salad to "make a palm tree" and daring her to "find the coconuts." Handling food may violate local health ordinances.

DON'T wear a blindfold. The logs of our hospital emergency wards are chock-full of such notations as "Walked into an electric fan," "baited a Rottweiler," "freak knothole accident." Our medical samaritans have far more urgent duties than treating Viagrans on a lark.

DON'T respond to the bankruptcy judge's request that you declare your assets by unzipping your fly. "Assets" in these proceedings are limited strictly to matters of financial worth. You could face fraud charges.

DON'T, when playing charades, pantomime the words "joystick" or "battering ram" or "Sears Tower" by turning sideways to your audience. Women cannot duplicate this gesture, and remember, not only may any "women's libbers" in attendance be offended, but a lot of them are now lawyers.

DON'T stand in queues. Nobody likes the "pushy" type.

VIAGRA: THE UNANSWERED QUESTIONS

The miracle of Viagra is still so new that science is not yet able to explain its every effect, or even the exact nature of its workings. We must wait to find the answers to these nagging conundrums:

◆ If Paul Shaffer takes Viagra, will David Letterman get an erection?

◆ If you take your first Viagra the night Kate Winslet agrees to sleep over, will you be unable to perform because you can't decide which action caused your tumescence?

◆ If you take three Viagra pills at once, will you experience multiple erections, or will a single erection pack the power of three?

◆ If Viagra emboldens you to ask Queen Elizabeth for a date and you "score," will you feel cheap and sordid afterward? If you choose to apologize, must you curtsy?

◆ If you are president and find Monica Lewinsky under your desk wearing kneepads, do you first call for a) Security; b) Scope; c) Viagra?

◆ If you are alone on a desert island and a crate of Viagra washes ashore, how will you commit suicide?

BEYOND VIAGRA'S REACH: THE EUNUCH SEX MANIAC

Meet Howard S. of Long Island, New York — not only the namesake and mascot but the living human inspiration behind Howard's House, a treatment center like no other in America.

Some day, Howard may be healthy enough to enjoy Viagra and its blessings. But not now. Howard was born with a Wadd Rating stuck at twenty-five times normal — far beyond the ability of sex to gratify his berserk urges. Forever feeling that he's about to explode, unable to think or talk of anything but sex for more than ten consecutive seconds, his world a swirling kaleidoscope of sexual imagery, Howard's condition is far worse than that of a sex slave. He is a *eunuch* sex slave.

Scientists at Howard's House hope that in the future a treatment will be available to shrink Howard's grotesquely distended sex glands, cool off his inflamed Wadd Rating and bring him within reach of the blessings of Viagra. Combining the "cold shower" principle with a saltpeter diet and such new technologies as a right-hand restraint harness with electric shock, researchers are already making progress in experiments with milder cases.

Meanwhile, prayers go forth for Howard and all the other Howards who dream that they too may one day share in the bounty of Viagra Nation.

ACKNOWLEDGMENTS

The authors wish to acknowledge the encouragement or forbearance of the following good women and men: our wives, Polly and Linda, who had the instinct to keep a safe distance from this project; our editor at HarperCollins, David Hirshey, who generously supplied us with bagels, news clippings, wisecracks and astute judgment on matters of taste and humor, not to mention the occasional services of his own reliable brain trust, Stanley Bing and Michael Solomon; Hans Teensma, so much more than an art director, who was uncommonly genial throughout this time-pressured experience; and finally, a personal physician – he shall remain nameless – who never doubted us for a second when we said we needed a hurry-up Viagra prescription because we were "writing a book."

The text of this book
was set in ITC Bodoni Six, a heavier
cut of Bodoni not meant to be used in larger sizes.
The display faces are Champion Featherweight, Middleweight,
Welterweight and Heavyweight "Extended."
Champion was designed by Jonathan Hoefler of the
Hoefler Typefoundry in New York City.

Design and production by
Impress, Inc.
Northampton, Massachusetts.